Henrik Hertz

King René's Daughter

A Danish lyrical drama

Henrik Hertz

King René's Daughter
A Danish lyrical drama

ISBN/EAN: 9783743408050

Manufactured in Europe, USA, Canada, Australia, Japa

Cover: Foto ©Thomas Meinert / pixelio.de

Manufactured and distributed by brebook publishing software (www.brebook.com)

Henrik Hertz

King René's Daughter

King René's Daughter

A DANISH LYRICAL DRAMA

BY

HENRIK HERTZ

TRANSLATED BY

THEODORE MARTIN

NEW YORK
LEYPOLDT & HOLT
1867

Entered, according to Act of Congress, in the year 1866, by

LEYPOLDT & HOLT,

in the Clerk's Office of the District Court of the United States for the Southern District of New York.

JOHN F. TROW & CO.,
PRINTERS, STEREOTYPERS, & ELECTROTYPERS,
50 GREENE STREET, N.Y.

PUBLISHERS' NOTICE.

It is surprising that the American press has issued so small a number of the foreign poems which are intimately known throughout Europe. There are many which have gone through several editions in each one of the principal European languages, English included, which have not been printed in America at all. The little poem herewith presented is as intimately known in England and Germany as almost any one in native literature. In the United States the only issue of it before the present, was a pamphlet printed—probably for stage uses—nearly twenty years ago.

In the hope of adding more of these foreign works to the American stock of good reading, we have already begun the preparation of "Frithiof's Saga," translated from the Swedish of Tegnér by Blackley, and edited, with a copious introduction and notes, by Bayard Taylor; also the "Nathan the Wise" of Lessing, with an introductory essay by K. Fischer—translated from the German by Miss Ellen Frothingham, of Boston.

If these great works meet with a favorable reception,

we will add others as long as the public taste shall warrant. Among those we have in contemplation are Goethe's "Hermann and Dorothea;" Molière's "Tartuffe;" Calderon's "Life is a Dream;" Tasso's "Aminta," translated by Leigh Hunt; "The Wooing of the King's Daughter," from the Norwegian of Munch; "Boris Godounoff," from the Russian of Pouschkine; "Nala and Damajanti," translated from the Sanscrit by Milman; and a translation of Bodenstedt's version of the Turkish songs of Mirza-Schaffy.

INTRODUCTORY SKETCHES.

I.—THE POET.

HENRIK HERTZ was born at Copenhagen, on the twenty-fifth of August, 1798. His parents were Jews. In 1817 he entered the law school of the Copenhagen University. While studying law with little interest, he was enthusiastically at work on general æsthetic studies, and especially on Persian literature. Though Hertz cared little for law, his works bear evidence that he probably owes much to it. The accurate framework of his writings, the just balance of his characters, and the ingenious construction of his scenes, would be natural to the very highest dramatic genius, but could hardly be wrought by a mind such as that of Hertz, unless its discriminative powers had received special culture. In spite of his attention to other things, he graduated creditably in law in 1825.

In 1826 he published, anonymously, his first work, *Herr Bughard og hans Familie*"—a comedy. This work bears unmistakable evidence of having been modelled on the comedies of Holberg, who, a century before, had infused the true catholic spirit into Danish literature. Hertz wrote about one play a year, publishing anonymously, until 1830, when he produced a queer poetical satire called "Letters of a Ghost" (*Gjenganger-breve*). It had the form of epistles from Paradise, and its principal objects of attack were the somewhat diverse ones of the bad literary taste and the snobbishness of the age. He especially assailed a school that he considered servile imitators of Oehlenschläger, and he was not prophet enough to refrain from disturbing Hans Christian Andersen, who was then just rising into fame. This satire produced a furore fit to be compared with that called forth by English Bards and Scotch Reviewers. No literary event in Denmark had produced such a stir since the quarrel between Baggessen and Oehlenschläger, about a quarter of a century before. In the same year with the satire, he published the first versified comedy in Danish literature. It is called "Cupid's Master-Stroke" (*Amors Geniestreger*). The form of the dialogue is the same as in the French classical drama. It was another great success. Despite all this, he worked on anonymously, and the Danes called him their Great Unknown. Not till 1832 did he claim the laurels which his works had been earning for him. In the same year he embraced Lutheranism.

In 1833 he was admitted to the "travelling pension," with which the Danish Government encourages the promising young men of the nation. During that year and the one succeeding, he travelled in Germany, France, and Italy, and seems to have done nothing in literature beyond gathering materials.

The next one of his works deserving special notice was "Svend Dyring's House," a tragedy in four acts, which appeared in 1837. This play excited universal praise, and is one of the best exponents of the modern Scandinavian genius. It has been translated at least twice into German, and was played at Berlin in 1849. "The Plumage of the Swan" (*Svanehammen*), a comedy in three acts (1841), also deserves to be considered a representative play.

In 1839 Hertz published a novel called "Characters and Circumstances" (*Stemninger og Tilstande*)—an interesting and well-constructed book, but the course of the story is too much interrupted by political disquisitions. These are of such a character, that, on the work's appearance, they called down upon the author severe attacks from the liberal press. Nevertheless, the book went through at least two editions.

KING RENÉ'S DAUGHTER appeared in 1845. Although in plot and structure far less ambitious than many of his other plays, it has merits that have seldom, if ever, been elsewhere combined in the same degree. It took its place in literature at once. It has been translated into German four times—once by Breseman, with the assistance of the author—and four times into English. It has been represented at leading theatres in Germany, Holland, Sweden, England, and the United States. A paraphrase of it, by Gustave Lemoine, has been played at Paris.

In 1848 Hertz produced *Federigo*, an opera in three acts, the music by H. Rung. In 1849, his comedy of "A Hundred Years," written after the manner of Aristophanes, failed at the Royal Theatre in Copenhagen through bad stage management.

In 1858 he produced a romance, which we allude to because its name was "John Johnson" (*Johannes Johnson*). He further paid his respects to the English in a one-act interlude called "The Penny Show" (*Perspektivkassen*)—a string of humorous doggerel, in which he caricatured the English court, not omitting Sir Robert Peel, or even Queen Victoria herself. The latest of his productions of which we can find any record, is "Adventures of a Fortune-Teller" (4 vols., Copenhagen, 1862).

His works, collected in fifteen volumes (1853–1865), comprise over forty titles in nearly all departments of imaginative literature. His signal successes have undoubtedly been his dramas. Although the one that gave him widest fame was neither brilliant comedy nor profound tragedy, he has been more than successful in both; his novels have had a favorable reception; and his lyric and didactic poems are permanently fixed in the literature of his native land.

In 1850 the Danish Government spontaneously appointed him to a literary professorship, with a comfortable pension, which he still enjoys. The fact that at the age of sixty-four he published a four-volume novel, proves that his declining years are vigorous and useful, and so gives the best reason to hope that they are happy.

II.—THE POEM.

The principal characters in KING RENÉ'S DAUGHTER are historical, and the political complication named in the play, was actually resolved in the manner there foreshadowed.

The "Good King René" was born about 1400, and in his childhood was betrothed to the daughter of that same Duke of Burgundy who was assassinated by the Duke of Orleans at the bridge of Montereau. The engagement was broken, and René married Isabella of Lorraine. She bore him six children, one of whom— Yolande—is the Iolanthe of our story. He was, as Hertz depicts him, a brave, generous, pious, and cultivated gentleman. Some of his literary works still exist, and we have the strong impression that we have heard of songs which are attributed to him being still sung in Provence.

Despite his quiet tastes, he had a turbulent life fighting the counts of Vaudemont for the succession in Lorraine, which he claimed through his wife. Once when he was a prisoner on parole, he offered to settle the dispute in the manner told in the play. The offer was accepted, and, after some delay, the arrangement was consummated. Not very long after, René's queen died. He loved her with his whole chivalrous soul, and her loss left him broken-hearted. Resigning the kingdom to his heir, he spent the rest of his life alternately with Margaret and Yolande, whose children were the blessing of his old age.

We can find no historical evidence that Yolande was blind. In making Iolanthe so, however, Hertz, by treating it as a state secret, has ingeniously obviated any violent contradiction of history.

On beginning these little sketches, we had no idea of attempting anything like criticism of the poem. But the critical reading we have since given it, has disclosed one or two beauties of construction not apt to strike one on a casual perusal. Perhaps we may indicate them without appearing to insult the acumen of our readers, or incurring the danger of lessening their pleasure, as one would be apt to in challenging attention to a perfectly obvious merit. But if there be any one disposed to follow us through a few words of criticism, we are more than half inclined to beg him to read the poem first, and then, if he will, return to our comments. To us the poem seems full of that perfect art which conceals art; and we do not wish to spoil the poet's success in covering over his framework, by pointing out beforehand places where our search has shown us something admirable in its structure.

Most readers who have been through the poem will probably be pleasantly surprised to reflect that it is all contained in a single act, and in a single stage-scene. Although informed of the fact at the outset, we confess to have lost sight of it entirely.

The perfectly peaceful, *lovely* character of the poem is maintained throughout with great art. Through such a complication of circumstances, Iolanthe's blindness is never made to shock the reader. Nine artists out of ten would have made her discovery of it a painful and agonizing scene. Hertz has not only provided the reader with an under-thought of satisfaction at her learning it, but has made the manner of her doing so inexpressibly lovely.

The whole piece is made to bear the beautifully unreal air of romance, by the ingenious interfusion of little bits of superstition, which, though entirely natural to the age, would have had an air of grossness in the hands of a clumsy artist.

The confidence with which Iolanthe welcomes Geoffrey and Tristan, indicates the master. At first it appears unnatural. But she did not know what unkindness was, and therefore did not fear it.

Geoffrey praises the wine. Tristan is so absorbed in Iolanthe that he does not notice it.

To the modern sense, Geoffrey's volunteering of the song, at first looks like a coarse stage-trick. On second thought, though, it must appear entirely in keeping with the spirit of an age when every gentleman carried his cithern, and the whole neighboring country felt the influence of the Troubadour King. The older knight's desire to show off his pupil, after he himself had finished, is a good stroke. Iolanthe's simple "Give me the cithern," is a better one.

The character of the three songs is really worthy of notice. Geoffrey's mainly enunciates general principles, suggested by the occasion. It is natural for the elderly man to think in that way, and, moreover, it is befitting the skill of the more accomplished poet. Tristan's song is simply a narrative of what, at the moment, has entire possession of his soul. Such a song, too, is within the range of the poetical novice. Iolanthe's song is a natural combination of the peculiarities of the other two. She is young enough to habitually think in particulars, and she is not, like Tristan, so wholly absorbed in any one immediate object as to prevent her thinking her habitual thoughts. Her experience is not, like Geoffrey's, old enough to be digested into intellectual generalities, but she draws upon it for special feelings.

And now we are able both practically to evince our regret at the growing disuse of a good old-fashioned habit, and to indulge our own hearty impulse, by wishing the reader much pleasure from the perusal of the poem itself. If, by taking our advice and reading the poem before proceeding this far in our introduction, he has made our good wishes seem tardy, we do not know that we can do better than to establish their propriety by advising him to read it again.

DRAMATIS PERSONÆ.

King René of Provence.
Iolanthe, his Daughter.
Count Tristan of Vaudemont.
Sir Geoffrey of Orange.

Sir Almerik.
Ebn Jahia, a Moorish Physician.
Bertrand.
Martha, his Wife.

———◆———

(The scene lies in Provence, in a valley of Vaucluse, and lasts from midday to sunset. Time—The middle of the fifteenth century.)

To the left (of the actor) stands a house of one story, covered with ivy and roses,—its windows shaded by verandahs. A garden runs backwards from the house, in which the vegetation displays a tropical luxuriance. Some date-palms in the foreground. At the end of the garden is seen a wall of rock, overgrown with brushwood, and in it a door so covered with moss and stones, that it is only perceptible when open. Behind this wall lofty mountains stretch into the distance.

KING RENÉ'S DAUGHTER.

FIRST SCENE.

BERTRAND. *Immediately afterwards*, SIR ALMERIK. *Then* MARTHA.

BERTRAND (*entering from the house*).
It was the bell! Some message from the king!
(*Crosses the stage to the rock, and opens the concealed door. Returns immediately with Sir Almerik, but keeps him standing at the entrance.*)
Sir Almerik! You here! Stand back! Nay, not a step!
No stranger enters here.

ALMERIK.
I must and will!

BERTRAND.

No, not a foot, by heav'ns! You have deceived me.
Hearing the bell, and with it, too, the sign,
I felt assured that it must be Raoul.

ALMERIK.

The king has sent me hither in his stead.
See here this letter, and his royal ring.

BERTRAND.

His ring? 'Tis so. A letter! By your leave?
(*Reads.*) " Frankly confide in Almerik, and give him
Whatever information he desires."
—This changes matters quite. Frown not, my lord;
For if you know the secret of this place,
Then you must know that prudence is my duty.

>ALMERIK (*advancing with Bertrand to the front of the stage*).

I know the place's secret? Save the mark!
I find myself here to my own surprise,
And all I see augments my wonderment.
A very paradise amid the waste!
Read me the mystery.

BERTRAND.

How! from the king
Did you not learn it?

ALMERIK.

Nay, not I!

BERTRAND.

So, so!
If he was silent, I must needs be dumb.

ALMERIK.

Nay, nay, you jest!

BERTRAND.

I never jested less.

MARTHA (*appearing at the door of the house*).
Sir Almerik?

BERTRAND.

He brings King René's ring,
And knows the sign to gain admittance here.
But nothing more. He must at once begone.

ALMERIK.

Begone, when the king sends me?

BERTRAND.

Ay, although he did.

MARTHA.

Stay, Bertrand, stay! (*To* ALMERIK.) What is your
message, sir?

ALMERIK.

I was to say, that in an hour the king
Would come with his physician, Ebn Jahia.

MARTHA.

The very famous Moor, I know him well——

ALMERIK.

Comes with the king, and you were to make sure—
These were his words—that all things were prepared
As the leech ordered you.

BERTRAND.

'Tis well—'tis well!
The king may trust to us. Some hours ago
Was Ebn Jahia here.

MARTHA.

And yet, Sir Knight,
His Majesty imparted nothing more?

ALMERIK.

He was in haste, and full, meseem'd, of thought.
The moor—this Ebn Jahia—had arrived,

Raoul was ill, and secretly the king
Call'd me aside. "I can depend on you,"
He said, "and in your secrecy confide!
Follow the messenger, who will conduct you,
And then fulfil your charge."

MARTHA.

And this was all
Was told you by the king?

ALMERIK.

Not all; and yet,
What more he spake was wrapp'd in mystery.
He mused awhile, then, hesitating, said:
"Look you! I count on your fidelity;
You'll find my daughter, where you are to go."
Then all at once he suddenly broke off,
Penn'd in keen haste the letter which I brought,
And bade me go.

MARTHA.

The letter?

BERTRAND.

Ah, yes! The letter!

MARTHA (*takes and reads the letter*).
'Tis the king's hand. How can you doubt his tale?

BERTRAND.

No, you are right; I had forgot the letter.

ALMERIK.

Then from the letter you may gather how
The king desires that from your lips I learn
What things soe'er 'tis needful I should know.
Who is this daughter that he told me of?
Margaret is now in Britain, and Iolanthe——

MARTHA.

Is here.

ALMERIK.

   Here? Iolanthe is in Spain,
Rear'd in a convent since her infancy.

MARTHA.

Not so, Sir Knight; she's here, and has been ever.

ALMERIK.

How? Here! I prithee, Bertrand, tell me all!

BERTRAND.

You oft, no doubt, have heard of the dispute
About **Lorraine**, that raged so long between
Our king and Vaudemont.

KING RENÉ'S DAUGHTER.

ALMERIK.

     I know it well.
Yet is that ancient quarrel now forgot.
The terms of peace, by Burgundy arranged,
Secure—as rumor gives the story out—
King René's daughter's hand in marriage to
The son of Count Antonio Vaudemont.
This daughter, Iolanthe, was a child
When this alliance was determined on.

BERTRAND.

'Twas even as you say; but, good Sir Knight,
The compact scarce was settled, when, by fire,
The palace was consumed at dead of night,
And Iolanthe—then a one year's babe—
Had all but perish'd in the flames. To save
Her life, one course, and one alone, was left:
We from the chamber window let her down,
And caught her safe on cushions as she fell.
Yet, or through fear or injury from the fall,
Suffice to say, the child had lost her sight.

ALMERIK.

Had lost her sight?

Martha.

                Ay, even so, my lord.
Imagine our distress—her sire's despair.
Alas! a child so gentle and so sweet,
And of her sight bereft—how sad! how hard!
The hope, that with her life was intertwined,
Extinguished, and the old and bitter feud
About Lorraine renewed—ay, and renewed
Too sure, alas! more fiercely than of old.
For the Count Vaudemont will never brook
His son should have a blind girl for his mate.
He will believe, and hence his wrath will fire,
A cheat was practised on him, and that she
Was blind before the truce was ratified.

Almerik.

Surmise to him most probable. But the king,
What did he in this strait?

Bertrand.

                    At first he veiled
In studious silence that the child was blind,
Which none had e'er discovered from her looks;
But soon from Cordova he summoned hither
The very famed physician, Ebn Jahia,

Whose skill is counted nigh miraculous,
Who came and tried all sorts of remedies.
With sagest counsel, too, he showed us how
To rear her up in tender fosterage;
And, last of all, he in the stars perused
Her horoscope.

     ALMERIK.

  And there?

     MARTHA.

       Found hope for us,
That Iolanthe should regain her sight
When in her sixteenth year. That time is come,
And Ebn Jahia now is with the king.
He orders remedies, which we apply,
Yet what their purpose I have never known;
The hour, he says, hath even now arrived.
Heaven grant it may be so!

     ALMERIK.

      But Iolanthe!
How heavily her fate must weigh her down!

     MARTHA.

She has no thought herself that she is blind.

ALMERIK.

No thought that she is blind! You surely jest!

MARTHA.

Ah, no, Sir Knight! you very soon may learn
That all which I have told you now is true.
But let me earnestly beseech you, sir,
When you converse with Iolanthe, still
To guard your lips with most religious care,
That so no syllable shall cross their bounds,
Which to the eye bears slightest reference.
This is the strict injunction laid on all
Who come within these precincts. Nothing name
Which through the power of vision must be known;
Speak not before her of the light of day,
Nor of the moonbeams in the placid night,
Nor of its thousand stars. Alas! no stars
Illume the lasting night wherein she dwells!

ALMERIK.

And have you kept subservience to this rule?

BERTRAND.

We school'd ourselves from her most tender years,
When there was little danger had we failed.

ALMERIK.

With what intent has it been hid from her
That she is blind? Who will'd it should be so?

MARTHA.

We know not whether 'twas the king's resolve,
Or whether Ebn Jahia so advised;
Yet I can easily explain the cause.
A coronet shall one day deck her brow,
As you are 'ware; so does her future hold
A brilliant promise forth, should all go well.
But it is feared the consciousness of blindness
Might settle deep into her tender soul,
Untune her spirit, and from her senses take
Their equipoise, and that clear cheerfulness,
Which are a throne's most beauteous ornaments.
This consciousness 'tis purposed to avert.

ALMERIK.

This is the reason, then, why she lives here,
Secluded from the world and all who might
Betray to her the secret of her loss?

BERTRAND.

'Tis even so. This valley, lock'd within
The heart of yonder mountains of Vaucluse,

Is from the eye of all intruders safe.
You know, it is King René's chief delight
To tend and cultivate his plants and flowers.
Thus all you see was by himself arranged,
And with the trees and shrubs his daughter grew.
Here knows she every spot,—unerringly
Can find her way about without a guide.
Nor has her education been o'erlook'd:
She weaves, spins, tends her garden-plots, and is
Forever occupied, and ever cheerful.
Songs makes she too, and sings at leisure hours.

ALMERIK.

Makes songs!

BERTRAND.

    Ay, she makes songs. The king himself
Taught her the cunning of the troubadours;
And ne'er a master of them all need blush
To own the verses which her fancy weaves.

ALMERIK.

All this I can explain and understand;
Yet how she ne'er suspects her blindness, I
Can scarce conceive. No—this must be delusion!

MARTHA.

Such it appears to you, whose eyesight serves
As a sure guide to every step you take.
Involuntarily you turn your gaze
Towards every sound that stirs. Even in the dark,
The accustomed light with fancied gleam deceives you;
But he, who from his earliest infancy,
From birth, mayhap, hath lack'd the power of sight,
How shall he deem his fellow-creatures see?
What's sight to him? What can he comprehend
Of all that wondrous power that's in the eye?
Yet, as with ease we master by its aid
All that surrounds us, so the blind do hold
Hearing, touch, feeling, the air's soft impress,
And other means innumerable, at command,
Which are to us incomprehensible.
—This shall yourself observe, as I have said,
Before you have been long with Iolanthe.

ALMERIK.

Now, by the mass, I long to see this wonder!
—Yet one thing more, that puzzles me, explain:
She lives alone with you, apart from all;
Is this secluded valley all her world?

BERTRAND.

You err, to think that Iolanthe is
So lonely, so forlorn. Behind these mountains
Lies, as you know, the convent of St. Clara;
And oftentimes the abbess and the nuns
Come here to visit her; her father, too,
Brings with him stranger-guests from time to time.

ALMERIK.

And so she lacks for nought, and is content
If but some stranger on occasion come?
Of all the wealth the world to us presents,
Of all its glories, she surmiseth nought?
Does she not question you?

MARTHA.

                        That is a point
On which 'tis not so easy to reply.
It may be she suppresses many a thought.
She knows there is an entrance to this vale,
Hears the bell sound when any one arrives,
Brightens to hear it, and in silence waits,
With ear intent. Yet doth she never ask
Where is the entrance, whitherward it leads;

For she has heard that there are many things
She must not ask, but leave to years to teach.

    So 'tis with children. Speak to them of God,
Of power omnipotent, of another life,
And mark how they will listen, opening wide
Their little eyes in wonder, as some doubt—
A passing shade—is painted on their looks;
And then, at last, with touching faith, accept
For truth the things they may not comprehend.
So now for Iolanthe the whole world
Is one vast mystery, which she oft would pierce.
Then will her father or the abbess say:
"Rest thee content, my child—thou art too young;
Some future time thou'lt comprehend it all."
In this she piously confides; nor dreams
She wants the eyes' clear sight, to compass all
The splendors of this goodly universe.
—May it not be, sir, while we darkly muse
Upon our life's mysterious destinies,
That we in blindness walk, like Iolanthe,
Unconscious that true vision is not ours?
Yet is that faith our hope's abiding star.

ALMERIK.

In this, good Martha, hast thou truly spoken.
But tell me, where is Iolanthe now?

BERTRAND.

She sleeps.

ALMERIK.

How! Sleeps! And now?

BERTRAND.

For just one hour,
By the physician's order, every day.
Yet 'tis no soft and natural sleep; indeed,
I'm puzzled sorely what to think of it.
By strange and uncouth words, and singular signs,
Does Ebn Jahia charm her to repose;
Then doth he place upon her breast a stone,
A talisman or amulet, belike,
And only when he has removed the gem,
Does she awake again. I will confess,
This troubles me.

ALMERIK.

Yet may we strongly trust
In Ebn Jahia's skill.

BERTRAND.

There lies my hope.

(*The bell rings.*)

MARTHA.

Bertrand, the bell!

BERTRAND.

Nay, then, it is the king.

(*Exit through the concealed door.*)

ALMERIK.

Comes the king often hither?

MARTHA.

Yes, when he
Has fixed his quarters at the neighboring palace,
We see him frequently. At times, however,
Whole months will pass without his coming here.

ALMERIK.

Knows Iolanthe, then, it is the king?

MARTHA.

No, she doth not, and that is well remembered.
She has no thought of that. She calls him father,
We others call him Raymbaud—such the name
Of one that was a famous troubadour.

ALMERIK.

Break off! The king!

SECOND SCENE.

KING RENÉ, EBN JAHIA, *and* BERTRAND *enter through the concealed door.* ALMERIK, MARTHA.

RENÉ.

Martha, I bring thee here
Good Ebn Jahia. As I learn, he hath
Been here to-day already once before.
How goes it now?

MARTHA.

Even to a wish, my liege.

RENÉ.

All that the leech enjoined thou hast fulfilled?
Neglected nothing? Has Iolanthe lain
With eyes close bandaged every night?

MARTHA.

She has.

RENÉ (*to* EBN JAHIA).

That was a perilous venture. It is strange
She bears it. Yet the chance was fortunate
That the bee stung her on the temple lately;
This served us for a plausible pretext.
Ah! sure the little bee deceived itself.
In this fair world, that's tended by her care,
Where, like a flower, she grows amidst her flowers,
The insect, dazzled by the flagrant bloom,
Deemed that it nestled in a rose's bud.
Forgive me! It is sinful thus to speak
Of mine own child. But now no more of this.
Thou long'st to see the fruitage of thy skill.
Go, then, to Iolanthe. Bertrand! Martha!
Follow him in; perchance he may require you.

(EBN JAHIA *exit into the house, followed by* BERTRAND *and* MARTHA.)

Now, Almerik, tell me, wert thou not amazed,
To see this valley, so serene and still?
Was it not so—a little paradise?

ALMERIK.

Indeed it is!

RENÉ.

Oh, had it been my fate,

Here, in the midst of all that most I love,
Of beauty, science, art, to spend my days,
How gladly, then, had I foregone, forever,
Naples, Lorraine, and this long, bitter strife
With Vaudemont!

ALMERIK.

              This strife is now heal'd up,
And you expect Count Tristan here ere long.
Then all shall end in peace.

RENÉ.

                  I hope it may!
And this my hope has daily gained in strength.
I told you—did I not?—that I expected
Geoffrey of Orange. He resided long
At Tristan's castle. The Count's teacher he
In minstrelsy, and poetry and song.
The youthful Count, so Geoffrey tells me, owns
A happy turn for poesy—a sense
Refined and gentle, with a mind of rare
Endowment and capacity of thought.
He sang to me a Sirventese, writ
By Tristan, nobly felt, and couch'd in words
Of a rare beauty. This I needs must own,

Though he be minded hostilely to me,
And would with grasping hand usurp Lorraine.
—But hush! I hear a voice.

(*Goes to the house and looks in at the door.*)

       See, Ebn Jahia
Has waken'd her! Slowly her eyes she raises;
She speaks—yet speaks as in a dream, while he
Looks down observantly into her eyes.
Now doth he lay the amulet once more
Upon her bosom—and she sleeps again.

     ALMERIK.

How singular!

     RENÉ.

   Most singular! This Moor
Possesses powers that fill me with alarm.
He comes. Now leave us, Almerik. Yet stay!
Hence to the palace. Here I must remain.
Soon as a letter comes from Tristan, haste
And bring it here to me.

     ALMERIK.

    Adieu, my liege.
(*Exit, as* EBN JAHIA *enters from the house.*)

RENÉ.

My Ebn Jahia, com'st thou like the dove
That bears the olive-branch? Thou lookest grave,
And, as thine art, unfathomable all.
How shall I construe what thy looks import?

EBN JAHIA.

I have the strongest hopes, my noble liege.

RENÉ.

Is't so? Oh, thou'rt an angel sent from heaven!
Thy dusky visage, like that royal Moor's
Who knelt beside our great Redeemer's cradle,
Heralds the star, shall cheer my night of gloom.
Say, Jahia, say, whereon thy hope is based?
What is thy counsel, what thy purpose? Speak!
'Tis written in a book, which late I read,
That oftentimes an unsound eye is cured
By application of the surgeon's knife.
This thou wilt never try, my Ebn Jahia;
Thou know'st the eye is a most noble part,
And canst not gain such mastery o'er thyself
As to approach my Iolanthe's eyes
With instrument of steel. Nay, thou must dread
To mar the beauty of their azure depths,

That dark, deep fount, which still, though sadden'd o'er,
Wells forth such glorious radiance. Oh! her eyes,
How is it possible that night should brood
On two fair orbs of such transcendent sheen?

EBN JAHIA.

Nay, be at ease! You need not fear for this.
'Twould aid us little, should I have recourse
To instruments.

RENÉ.

What is thy purpose, then?

EBN JAHIA.

Your pardon, good my lord! My treatment is
A mystery, like all my leech's craft;
It scarce would serve my purpose to divulge it.
'Tis not the fruitage of a moment's growth;
No, but the slow result of wakeful years,
Shaped—step by step conducted to one point,
Whereat, so speed it Heaven! it shall succeed;
Ay, and succeed it must, this very day,
Or fail forever.

RENÉ.

How! This very day?

EBN JAHIA.

Soon as the sun has sunk beneath the hills,
And a soft twilight spreads along the vale,
Such as her eyes, still to the light unused,
May bear with safety, I will test my plan.

RENÉ.

Ah, Ebn Jahia, prithee, not to-day!
From day to day, from hour to hour, have I,
With restless eagerness, look'd onwards for
This moment; and alas! now it hath come.
My heart grows faint, and wishes it away.
—Think what I peril! When the sun goes down,
My fairest hope, perchance, goes down with it.
Thou'rt wrapt in thought. Art thou content to pause?

EBN JAHIA.

I will not wait.

RENÉ.

Then tell me, dost thou fear?
Art thou not certain of the issue? Thou
Didst put to question yonder silent stars,
From which thy potent art can wring response.
What was their answer? tell me, Ebn Jahia.
The horoscope—was't happy?

EBN JAHIA.

Yes, it was.
I told you so already. Yet the stars
Inclinant, non necessitant. They influence
The fortunes of mankind, yet do they not
Rule Nature's laws with absolute control.
Rest thee at ease : I have no fear for this.
—Another hindrance menaces my skill.

RENÉ.

A hindrance ?

EBN JAHIA.

One, my liege, I apprehend,
Which you will find it hard to obviate.
Iolanthe, ere I bend me to my task,
Must comprehend what she till now has lack'd—
Must learn this very day that she is blind.

RENÉ.

No, Ebn Jahia, no ; this cannot be !

EBN JAHIA.

It must be, or my skill is powerless.

RENÉ.

No, no ! oh, never ! never ! Thou wilt not

Constrain me to this monstrous cruelty,
And strip her all at once, with sudden wrench,
Of that unconsciousness has been her blessing;
Not slowly, by degrees, but all at once,
Force on her tender soul this fearful truth?
And if the cure should fail us after all?
Hast thou forgot how we, year after year,
With care almost incredible, have watch'd
To keep from her this melancholy truth?
This course thyself suggested—showing me
The difficult road which I was bound to follow.
Now, wilt thou raze the fabric thou hast reared?
Say, wherefore—wherefore?

EBN JAHIA.

                     I will tell you wherefore,
So please you lend a favoring ear the while.
You deem, belike, our sense of vision rests
Within the eye; yet is it but a means.
From the soul's depths the power of vision flows,
And those fine nerves, that on the eye converge,
From the brain's secret workshop emanate.
Iolanthe must be conscious of her state—
Her inward eye must first be opened, ere

The light can pour upon the outward sense.
A want must be developed in her soul;
A feeling that anticipates the light—
A craving sense; for know, my noble liege,
That nothing e'er is on mankind bestowed,
Unless for it he feel necessity.
Deep in his soul a yearning must arise
For a contentment, which it strives to win.
Let me, for you, exemplar take from what
Your studies make familiar. That fair art—
That joyous science of sweet poesy,
Which is so widely famed throughout Provence—
Mankind receive it by the Muses' favor:
Is it not so? But how? Do all receive it?
No; only he within whose bosom dwelt,
As in a dream, a bright poetic world,
And who hath yearned for it with quenchless love.

René.

I'll not contest with thee, good Ebn Jahia!
I may not cope with thee in lore profound;
Yet pity's voice speaks loudly in my heart,
And drowns thy arguments with mightier tones.
I cannot do it! No, it may not be!

EBN JAHIA.

E'en as you will. I only can advise ;
And if you will not trust to my advice,
Then I am useless here. So, fare ye well!
Hence to the convent, I ! There you will find me,
If your resolve shall alter. Yet, bethink you :
Sink but the sun behind yon mountain tops,
My utmost skill cannot again avail.

    (*Exit through the concealed door.*)

RENÉ.

Oh, dreadful strait ! And I so dearly bought
A hope, which yet so soon may be undone !
Shall I destroy at once her cheerful mood,
Convert it into comfortless despair,
And see her youth grow pale by slow degrees,
Wither and die in mournful consciousness ?
No ! This is Jahia's obstinacy merely ;
He yet shall yield. I will not rest until
He hears me, and submits to my desire.

    (*Exit after* EBN JAHIA, *as* MARTHA *and*
    BERTRAND *enter.*)

MARTHA.

The king gone hence, and, as it seemed, in wrath,

And Ebn Jahia nowhere to be seen!
What has occurred?

    BERTRAND.

      Indeed, Heav'n only knows!
Yet am I ill at ease, as matters stand:
And Ebn Jahia, I do fear me much,
Will fail us at the last.

    MARTHA.

    Nay, think ye so?

    BERTRAND.

Heaven grant that I be wrong! Yet like I not
The dark and moody nature of the man;
And, to be frank with you, I feel a dread
Of one endow'd with such mysterious pow'r.
There lies the child upon her couch, as though
Life were extinct; one motion of his hand,
And sleep, as if by magic, seals her eyes.
This is not, cannot come to good!

    MARTHA.

      Content thee,
Nor thus torment thyself with causeless fears.
Thou knowest well, that when her sleep is o'er,

And from her breast the amulet removed,
She beams afresh in bright and blooming health.
Is it not marvellous, how this strange sleep
Strengthens her more, much more, than sleep at night—
Gives vigor, and enlivens every sense?
Yea, ev'n her eyes, as I have noted oft,
Are deepen'd in their lustre when she wakes,
As though the rays of light had found a way
Into their orbs, while she lay slumbering:
This is, I trust, a favorable sign.

BERTRAND.

Well, well, thou may'st be right; and time will show!—
Let us away! Much yet is to be done
Among our people yonder in the field.
We may withdraw from Iolanthe now:
She sleeps, and cannot wake till our return.
(*Exeunt behind the house.*)

THIRD SCENE.

TRISTAN *of Vaudemont*, GEOFFREY *of Orange, each with a cithern slung upon his shoulder.*

GEOFFREY (*stopping in front of the concealed door*).
Look to your steps! 'tis dark as midnight here!

TRISTAN.
Push onward! Stay—here is a door!

GEOFFREY.
A door?

TRISTAN.
Patience! A bolt—it yields! What do I see?
(*Both enter.*)

GEOFFREY.
Heavens! What a gust of exquisite perfume!

TRISTAN.
A garden! Here—shrined in the mountain waste!
What beauty, too—what order! Only look!

GEOFFREY.
I am amazed!

TRISTAN.

What man is he, that owns
This witching spot? You know the country well,
And dwell hard by.

GEOFFREY.

Indeed, I cannot say.
Of such a paradise I never dreamed.
A garden of the tropics—studded o'er
With all rare flowers! Behold the lofty palms!

TRISTAN.

The mansion rising through—how beautiful!
Half-hid with ivy and the clambering rose!
—And yet, its inmates?

GEOFFREY.

Not a soul see I.
I could be sworn, this paradise arose
In some fair summer night, when Dian gave
One golden hour to her Endymion,
Veiling beneath these rocks their fearful joys!
But its inhabitants have taken flight.

TRISTAN.

Nay, here be many signs of human hands,

Fair, I'll be sworn, and gentle. Here—see here
Fresh footmarks on the pathway!

Geoffrey.

You are right.
A tiny foot and dainty! Let us on!
By following this we scarce can go amiss.
Observe, it leads right onwards to the house!

Tristan.

No, let us wait till somebody appears.
We should be most discourteous. Bad enough,
That we have come thus far without consent!

Geoffrey.

Well, as you please. So our luck fails us not,
I'll tax my courtesy, and wait in patience,
For, in good sooth, luck hath been ours indeed—
Hath it not, Tristan? See, how things have fallen:
As near the convent idly on we stroll'd,
Whiling the time with interchange of song,
I chanced to spy King René passing near,
Rapt in close talk with the Cordovan leech.
To 'scape his glance, you drag me after you,
And, hurrying on o'er rock and wilderness,

Here, at the mountain's base, we chance upon
Yon secret passage, craftily contrived.
Following it up, awhile we grope about
In darkness, and, in short, have landed here.
—But tell me, now, what prompted you
So to avoid the king? To meet him, 'twas,
That you came here. You urged me to attend
Upon you at the interview to-morrow;
And you—'tis known familiarly to all—
You have been long affianced to his daughter.

TRISTAN.

Affianced! Yes, they say so. Yet was I
Scarce nine years old, when I was thus betrothed.
My father made the terms with Burgundy,
When we a truce concluded with the king
But, Geoffrey, now I'm grown to riper years;
And as this contract, in the full career
Of victory, wrong'd and robb'd me of my rights,
So on this marriage look I now with hate.
Unwillingly I came; unwillingly
In this vile business I am like to move.

GEOFFREY.

I grieve to hear it, for King René's sake.

For many a day, I know, his joy has been
The goodly promise of these nuptial ties.

TRISTAN.

Goodly to him they may be, I believe.
—Know you his daughter?

GEOFFREY.

      No; she has been rear'd
In some far Spanish convent, and came home
Here to her father, but to meet with you.
—But let us, friend, bethink us where we are!
We forced our way in, and, it must be own'd,
The spot is charming. But the question now,
Is, can we quite as easily retire?

TRISTAN.

Nay, never fear.

GEOFFREY.

    Would you not, then, find out
Whether this mansion hath inhabitants?
Assail the door!—Shall I, then?

TRISTAN.

       Nay, let me!
In case some demon lord it in this place.

'Tis just, the danger first should light on me,
Whose charge it was that lured you on to it.

(*Knocks at the door.*)

No—no one comes!

GEOFFREY.

Try if the door will open.

TRISTAN.

It gives not way.

GEOFFREY.

Press harder; it will yield!

TRISTAN.

So be it, then! (*Opens the door.*) Heavens, Geoffrey, what a form!

GEOFFREY.

Some spirit?

TRISTAN.

How! A spirit? Yes, methinks
One of the radiant ministers of light!
Look!

GEOFFREY (*looking in*).

A fair girl upon a dainty couch!
Surely she sleeps!

TRISTAN.

      She sleeps. Her breathing heaves
Her bosom gently—gently sinks it down.
See, now a smile is hovering on her lips,
As though she dreamt of our bewilderment.

GEOFFREY.

I pray you, Tristan, let us fly from hence!
This witching vision doth disturb my soul—
Too witching all, and all too beautiful.
This is some wizard's castle—let us away!
Come! Mystic serpents threaten us, I know.
—Tristan, where are you rapt? All heavenly powers!
He's charm'd already! Rooted to the earth,
He stands, and stares on her. Oh, Tristan, come!

TRISTAN.

Speak softly, Geoffrey, for a breath might wake her!
Speak softly! 'Twere a sin to break the calm,
The holy stillness, which her slumber sheds
On everything around!

GEOFFREY.

      Oh, hear me! hear me!

TRISTAN.

Hush! Not a word, I say! This place is holy!

(Kneels, bending forward with outstretched arms towards the open door.)

Oh, be not angry, that with eyes profane
I have intruded on thy resting-place!

GEOFFREY.

Rise up! I tremble for you! You are caught
In an enchanter's spell. The vision is
Some cheating phantom. Follow me!

TRISTAN.
          I cannot.
GEOFFREY.

Then do not kneel there like a marble block!
Tush! be a man. If hence you will not fly,
At least command your spirits! Let us learn
Who this fair creature is. Awake her!

TRISTAN.
          No!

That were a sin!

GEOFFREY.
   If you will not, I will. *(Enters.)*

TRISTAN.

Audacious man! He calls to her—hark! hark!
How now—he clasps her hand——

GEOFFREY (*rushing out*).

      Away! away!
She cannot wake. Her senses are enthrall'd
By some dark demon's necromantic spells.
Oh, come! I quake for fear! We've rudely broke
Into a holy place—'twill be our death!

TRISTAN.

A holy place! You name it well. But it
Imports not death, but life. Well, well, no matter!
Come, let us quit this consecrated ground,
Which wrongly we intruded on. She sleeps.
It is unchivalrous to tarry——

GEOFFREY.

      Come!

TRISTAN.

Yet stay! I'll grant myself one little look,
One moment by her side, to scan her face,
Then follow you anon.   (*Enters.*)

GEOFFREY.

    See there—he kneels!
Upon her hand imprints one gentle kiss.
How he surveys her! There—he hath unclasp'd

A ribbon from her neck, and bears it off!
Now, Heav'n be praised, he comes to me again.

    TRISTAN (*returns*).

Now have I graven deeply on my heart
Her beauteous form. It cannot vanish now.
Ay, let us hence, and dread this witchery!
Yet did I vow to seek this spot again,
And, if I err'd not, with a gracious smile
She heard my vow, and bless'd it in her dreams.
See, Geoffrey, I have ta'en this ornament,
A gem of price, that lay upon her breast.
Like Jesse's son, who from the sleeping Saul
Took of his robe a fragment, for a sign
That in his hands the monarch's life had been,
So may this jewel likewise testify
That I was here, and that my life was placed
Within her hand, even while she lay in sleep.
Come, Geoffrey!

   (*Returns with* GEOFFREY *towards the concealed door, as* IOLANTHE *appears at the door of the house.*)

FOURTH SCENE.

Tristan. Geoffrey. Iolanthe.

(*Notwithstanding* Iolanthe's *blindness, all her movements are unconstrained and decided. Only now and then a listening attitude, with a slight motion of the hand, as though she were feeling before her, betrays the want of sight. Her eyes are open, but frequently bent downwards, and with little motion in them.*)

Iolanthe (*at the door*).
Martha! Bertrand!

Tristan.
Ha! 'tis she!

Iolanthe.
Sure, some one spoke! (*Advances.*) Who's there?

Tristan.
A stranger, who
Implores forgiveness, that he rudely broke
Your and this place's sanctified repose.

Iolanthe.
Give me thy hand. Thou never hast been here!

Nor do I even know thy voice. Didst speak
With Bertrand or with Martha on the way?

TRISTAN.

I spoke with no one. Accident alone
Hath led me hither.

GEOFFREY (*aside to* TRISTAN).

Ask about Bertrand!

IOLANTHE (*listening*).

And whom hast thou brought with thee?

TRISTAN.

'Tis my friend,
A troubadour and knight, who dwells hard by.

IOLANTHE.

You both are truly welcome. Will you not
Go in with me? 'Tis cool and fresher there.

GEOFFREY (*quickly*).

Nay, so you please, we'll tarry where we are.
(*Aside to* TRISTAN.) 'Tis safer so, methinks!

IOLANTHE (*still holding* TRISTAN'S *hand*).

Thy hand is warm—
I feel the pulse's throb. Hath not the heat
Oppressed thee by the way? Art thou not thirsty?

Wait, and I'll bring thee forth a cup of wine.

(*Goes into the house.*)

Tristan.

Oh, what a lovely being ! What dignity,
What gracious gentleness in every feature !
And her sweet voice !

Geoffrey.

A wondrous voice, indeed !
That fascinates the heart at unawares,
And binds it utterly in softest thrall !
Of noble birth she is, beyond all question ;
Yet—some precaution cannot be amiss.
Drink not the wine, dear Tristan, when it comes.

Tristan.

I would drink death, if from her hand, with joy !

(Iolanthe *comes back with a flagon and cup.*)

Iolanthe.

Here is the wine my father always drinks.
It is too strong for me ; but will you taste it ?

(*Fills the cup and presents it to* Tristan.)

Tristan (*as he drinks*).

This to thy happiness, thou lovely maid !

IOLANTHE.

Give now thy friend the cup, if he desire it.
I will go gather fruit for you—some dates
And grapes, or any other fruit you will.

   (*Plucks fruit, and places it in a basket which
   she has taken from the table.*)

  TRISTAN (*giving* GEOFFREY *the cup*).
There, Geoffrey, drink!

    GEOFFREY.

      Have you felt nothing strange—
No lassitude—no ——?

    TRISTAN.

     Nothing. Never fear!

    GEOFFREY.

It *is* wine, then? (*Drinks.*) Right Malvoisie, by
 heav'ns!
No better drinks King René's self, I trow.

      (*Drinks again.*)

Ha, what a wine! Where we such nectar find,
In sooth, no demon can have mastery!

   IOLANTHE (*rejoins them*).

Here I have fruits, so please you taste of them.
I'll place them on the table.

Geoffrey.

      Beauteous lady,
Already you so truly have refresh'd us,
And in this cup have minister'd a wine
So rare, and so delicious, we might deem,
And with best cause, our entertainment came
From some most wealthy, ay, and noble house.
Beauty and wine the loadstars are of song.
Then lend a friendly ear unto my words,
Which, lightly woven into a lay, unfold
At once our homage and our gratitude.
   (*Sings, accompanying himself on his cithern.*)

    The eagle we tell
    By his sweep full well,
As proudly afar in the clouds he soars;
    And the nightingale
    By the trilling wail
Her throat in the dewy May-time pours.

    By valor and skill,
    And a temperate will,
The knight approveth his worth to all;

   And deftly to sing,
   With sweet minstrelling,
Makes troubadour honor'd in bower and hall.

  (*Changes the measure.*)
But when amid gentles and ladies gay,
  His echoing harp he raises,
And seeks by the flow of his tuneful lay
  To win him their guerdons, their praises;
And when with the goblet the foot-page fine
  His carol hath cheerly greeted,
Full soon doth he note, by the noble wine,
  'Neath a noble's roof he's seated.

    IOLANTHE.
The song is beautiful, and doth bespeak
A cunning high and rare.

    TRISTAN.
      My friend is famed
Among Provence's young troubadours.

   IOLANTHE (*to* TRISTAN).
Art thou, too, gifted with the power of song?

    TRISTAN.
Ah, I am but a novice; yet, methinks

Your gentleness doth make me bold to sing.
Then pray you for the deed accept the will.

    (Sings, preluding each verse with a few notes of the cithern.)

I came where the echoing city lay,
  And over the mountains I took my way,
Weary and darkling, by rock and by lea;
  When a valley burst suddenly on my sight,
  Basking and beaming in sunshine bright,
And gemm'd with all beautiful flowers that be.

Here all was still. No sweet bird's note
  On my listening ear in the silence smote—
No sound, or of man or of life arose;
  And, as in some temple's most sacred hall,
  In this vale of enchantment fair seem'd all
To be lull'd for aye in a charm'd repose.

A door flew wide, and a form of light
  Beam'd, like a star, on my wondering sight;
Like a dewy rosebud, oppress'd with sleep,
  Which a wizard's wand had over it thrown,
  Didst thou seem to me, thou lovely one,
And all things anear thee a hush did keep.

The zephyr dreams on thy pearly cheek,
The flame on the hearth burns faint and weak,
The palm-trees drowsily droop their crest;
  For all things have life through thee alone,
  For all things will only be thine own,
And close their eyelids when thine do rest.

Thou didst awake, and a soul of life,
Through air, and through flower and grove, grew rife,
As though a sunbeam their sleep had broke!
  Oh, gentle rose, take to thy heart,
  As the homage pure of my faltering art,
The lay which thy beauty to being woke!

IOLANTHE.

(*To* TRISTAN, *after a pause, in which she stands absorbed, with her hand upon her forehead.*)

Lend me the cithern.

(*After preluding upon the instrument, she sings, accompanying herself with occasional chords.*)

    Highly be honor'd
    The stranger guest,
    Who comes with a blithesome

And cordial heart,—
Brings us a treasure
Of story and measure,
And fills us with silent and wondering pleasure!

Yet higher than all
Be honor to him,
The guest who doth bring us
Song link'd to the lyre;
Who living thoughts, woven
In melody, pours,
And on wingèd words freely and joyously soars!

With the minestrel enters
An influence holy
Under our portals;
While that he singeth,
Listens the air,
Hush'd are the flowerets,
And, lowly inclining,
Stay their sweet breathing to list to the strain.

You, O ye strangers,
You who came hither

With harp and with song,
With me dividing
Your souls' inspiration,
You do I thank!
Ah! I so feeble,
I could not fathom
All that you sang.
Novel and strange,
Strange as yourselves,
It swept me along, the light-wingèd song;

Here in the valley,
Deep in the thicket,
Oftentimes nestleth
A stranger bird;
And in the evening,
Dream-like and still,
Her song from the leaves doth the nightingale trill.

No one can teach me
To sweep the guitar,
Till it throbs like her song.
No one can give me
Her rapturous strain,
That lifted my soul on its pinions, again.

Whence, O ye strangers,
Cometh your song?
Say, is its home there,
Where, as I deem,
Fond aspirations,
Yearning and sighs,
In the slumberous silence of evening arise?

Say, have the airy
Tenants of ether
Taught you their strains?
Strains so enchanting,
Flowing so wildly;
Strains that have freighted
My dreams with delight;
Strains full of story,
Life-like and clear;
Strains that gave glory
To all that is near!

    GEOFFREY.

What lofty poesy!

   TRISTAN (*to* IOLANTHE).
   To the nightingale
You have compared our song. Oh, were I but

The meanest, tiniest of yonder birds,
That build their nests anigh your dwelling-place,
And evermore might list the lovely strains
That do inspire your breast!

GEOFFREY.

                      Oh, noble lady,
There is one question—pray you pardon it!—
Which musing wonder forces to my lips:
You live here from the world cut off, and none
Of all the knights and ladies of Provence
Your rare perfections e'er have heard or known;
What line so blest can claim you for its child—
And who your father?

IOLANTHE.

                 How! Not know my father?
That gives me wonder; for none e'er come here
Who know not him.

GEOFFREY.

                I pray you, what his name?

IOLANTHE.

The rest do call him Raymbaud.

GEOFFREY.

Raymbaud? Raymbaud?
Is he a knight?

IOLANTHE.

A knight?

GEOFFREY.

Or warrior?
Wears he a helm, and shield, and golden spurs?
What his pursuits?

IOLANTHE.

That have I ne'er inquired.

GEOFFREY.

Why are you pent up here so close?

IOLANTHE (*surprised*).

So close?

GEOFFREY.

Ay, close and lonely?

IOLANTHE.

Lonely I am not.
There you do much mistake.

GEOFFREY.

Yet no one's here?

IOLANTHE.

No, no one's here. You're right; I cannot guess
How this should be. I never am alone.
But only wait, and I will summon Bertrand.
He will be truly glad that you are come.

(*Exit into the house.*)

GEOFFREY.

Now 'twill be seen who is this valley's lord.
Yet can I not subdue the rising thought,
That some dark mystery is here on foot,
Which he that owns this valley will be loath
That we should pry into. You cannot fail
To note, how cunningly yon door is covered
With moss, and stones, and branches, that, when closed,
It scarce may be distinguished from the rock.
Take my advice, and tarry near the door.
I will but wait till some one comes, and then
Betake me straightway to the mountain pass,
To keep the entrance clear for our escape.
Some of your people I may chance to meet.
Should aught appear amiss, I will return
Upon the moment. Do you hear me, Tristan?

TRISTAN.

Ay, ay! Go, go! There!

GEOFFREY.

      Is your heart enchain'd?
Has this young beauty quite enchanted you?

TRISTAN.

No, I am ill at ease. My head's confused;
I almost think this tranquil valley is
That goal for which I've panted all my days;
That here, at length, my restless, soaring pride
Shall find its true repose.

GEOFFREY (*gravely*).

      I prithee, friend,
Remember, that King René waits for you.

TRISTAN.

What is King René, or his hopes, to me?
What! For a province, which by law and right
Is truly mine, by our good swords achieved,
Shall I, in my youth's holiday, be chain'd
To his daughter—to a girl whom no one knows—
Whom no one e'er hath seen—whilst I——

GEOFFREY.

You rave!
This fit will pass. But now you are bewitch'd.
Stifle this feverish passion in your breast.

TRISTAN.

Could I do that, I were bewitch'd indeed.

GEOFFREY.

Hush! hush! Some one approaches.

(IOLANTHE *returns from the house.*)

IOLANTHE.

Are you here?

GEOFFREY.

Wilt lead us to the master of the house?

IOLANTHE.

Alas! they are all gone, and no one came
In answer to my call. They have forsook me.

TRISTAN.

But they will come again.

IOLANTHE.

Yes; thou art right—
They have gone forth, I warrant, to the vintage.

I, too, at times go with them. But, when not,
There still is some one with me.

    GEOFFREY (*to* TRISTAN).
        You stay here?
    TRISTAN.
I will.
    GEOFFREY.
So be it, while I go watch the pass.
(*Exit, bowing to* IOLANTHE, *who does not return the salutation.*)

    IOLANTHE (*listening*).
Goes thy friend hence?
    TRISTAN.
      He will return anon.
Your pardon now—let me atone a fault
I have committed; but oh, chide me not!
As you lay sleeping, from your breast I took
An ornament, as a memorial token.
'Tis here!
    IOLANTHE.
  Where? where?
    (TRISTAN *gives her the amulet.*)
     An ornament—and mine?

TRISTAN.

Yes; I conjecture so.

IOLANTHE.

It is not mine;
But I will ask of Martha.

    (*Lays the amulet on the table.*)

TRISTAN.

    In its stead
Pray give me one of yonder blushing roses,
That rear their petals, fairest 'mongst all flow'rs,
As though they were the counterfeit of thee!

IOLANTHE.

A rose? Oh, willingly!

    (*Plucks and gives him a white rose.*)

TRISTAN.

    Ah, it is white!
Give me the red one, that is fair as thou!

IOLANTHE.

What meanest thou?—a red one?

TRISTAN (*pointing*).

    One of these.

IOLANTHE.

Take it thyself!

TRISTAN.

No ; let me keep the rose
Which thou hast chosen, which thy fair hand has
   gather'd.
And in good sooth I do applaud thy choice.
For the white rose, within whose calyx sleeps
A faint and trembling ruddiness, betypes
The dream-like beauty of this garden fair.
Give me another rose—a white one, too ;
Then with the twin flowers will I deck my cap,
And wear them as thy colors evermore.

IOLANTHE (*plucks and gives him a red rose*).

Here is a rose ; meanest thou one like this ?

TRISTAN (*starts*).

I ask'd thee for a white rose.

IOLANTHE.

Well, and this?

TRISTAN.

Why this?—(*Aside.*) What thought comes o'er me ?
  (*Aloud.*) Nay, then, tell me (*holds up the two*

roses, along with another which he has himself gathered)

How many roses have I in my hand?

IOLANTHE (*stretches out her hand towards them*).
Give me them, then.

TRISTAN.
Nay, tell me without touching.

IOLANTHE.
How can I so?

TRISTAN (*aside*).
Alas! alas! she's blind!
(*Aloud, and with a faltering voice.*)
Nay, I am sure you know?

IOLANTHE.
No; you mistake.
If I would know how anything is shaped,
Or what its number, I must touch it first.
Is not this clear?

TRISTAN (*confused*).
Yes, certainly; you're right.
And yet sometimes——

IOLANTHE.
Well, well?—sometimes? Speak! speak!

TRISTAN.

I think there are——that there are certain things
Which we distinguish by their hues alone,
As various kinds of flowers, and various stuffs.

IOLANTHE.

Thou mean'st by this their character, their form;
Is it not so?

TRISTAN.

Nay, not exactly that.

IOLANTHE.

Is it so hard, then, to distinguish flowers?
Are not the roses round, and soft, and fine,
Round to the feeling, as the zephyr's breath,
And soft and glowing as a summer's eve?
Are gilliflowers like roses? No; their scent
Bedizzies, like the wine I gave to thee.
And then a cactus—are its arrowy points
Not stinging, like the wind when frosts are keen?

TRISTAN.

(*Aside.*) Amazement! (*Aloud.*) Have they never
 told thee, then,
That objects, things, can be distinguish'd, though
Placed at a distance,—with the aid—of sight?

IOLANTHE.

At distance? Yes! I by his twittering know
The little bird that sits upon the roof,
And, in like fashion, all men by their voice.
The sprightly steed whereon I daily ride,
I know him in the distance by his pace,
And by his neigh. Yet—with the help of sight?
They told me not of that. An instrument
Fashion'd by art, or but a tool, perhaps?
I do not know this sight. Canst teach me, then,
Its use and purpose?

TRISTAN (*aside*).

O almighty powers!
She does not know or dream that she is blind.

IOLANTHE (*after a pause*).

Whence art thou? Thou dost use so many words
I find impossible to understand;
And in thy converse, too, there is so much
For me quite new and strange! Say, is the vale
Which is thy home so very different
From this of ours? Then stay, if stay thou canst,
And teach me all that I am wanting in.

TRISTAN.

No, O thou sweet and gracious lady, no!
I cannot teach what thou art wanting in.

IOLANTHE.

Didst thou but choose, I do believe thou couldst.
They tell me I am tractable and apt.
Many, who erewhile have been here, have taught me
Now this, now that, which readily I learn'd.
Make but the trial. I am very sure
Thou hat'st me not. Thy tones are mild and gentle.
Thou wilt not say me "nay," when I entreat.
Oh, speak! I'm all attention when thou speakest.

TRISTAN.

Alas! attention here will stead thee little.
Yet—tell me one thing. Thou hast surely learn'd
That of thy lovely frame there is no part
Without its purpose, or without its use.
Thy hand and fingers serve to grasp at much;
Thy foot, so tiny as it is, with ease
Transports thee wheresoe'er thy wishes point;
The sound of words, the tone, doth pierce the soul
Through the ear's small and tortuous avenues;
The stream of language gushes from thy lips;

Within thy breast abides the delicate breath,
Which heaves, unclogg'd with care, and sinks again.

IOLANTHE.

All this I've noted well. Prithee, go on.

TRISTAN.

Then tell me, to what end dost thou suppose
Omnipotence hath gifted thee with eyes?
Of what avail to thee are those twin stars,
That sparkle with such wondrous brilliancy,
They scorn to grasp the common light of day?

IOLANTHE (*touches her eyes, then muses for a little*).

You ask of what avail?—how can you ask?
And yet, I ne'er have given the matter thought.
My eyes! my eyes! 'Tis easy to perceive.
At eve, when I am weary, slumber first
Droops heavy on my eyes, and thence it spreads
O'er all my body, with no thought of mine,
As feeling vibrates from each finger's tip.
Thus, then, I know my eyes avail me much.
And hast not thou experience had enough,
Wherein thine eyes can minister to thee?
Only the other morn, as I was planting

A little rosebush here, a nimble snake
Leapt out and bit me in the finger; then
With the sharp pain I wept. Another time,
When I had pined for many tedious days,
Because my father was detain'd from home,
I wept for very gladness when he came!
Through tears I gave my bursting heart relief,
And at mine eyes it found a gushing vent.
Then never ask me, unto what avail
Omnipotence hath gifted me with eyes.
Through them, when I am weary, comes repose;
Through them my sorrow's lighten'd; and through them
My joy is raised to rapture.

TRISTAN.

      Oh, forgive me!
The question was most foolish; for in thee
Is such an inward radiancy of soul,
Thou hast no need of that which by the light
We through the eye discern. Say, shall I deem
That thou of some unheard-of race art sprung,
Richly endow'd with other powers than we?
Thou livest lonely here—this valley, too,
Seems conjured forth by magic 'mongst the hills.

Hast thou come hither from the golden East,
With Peris in thy train?—Or art thou one
Of Brahma's daughters, and from Ind hast been
Transported hither by a sorcerer?
O beautiful unknown! if thou be'st sprung
Of mortal men, who call the earth their mother,
Be thou to life's so transitory joys
Susceptible as I, and deign to look
With favor on a knight's devoted love!
Hear this his vow: No woman shall efface
(Stand she in birth and beauty ne'er so high)
The image thou hast stamp'd upon my soul!

   IOLANTHE (*after a pause*).
Thy words are laden with a wondrous power.
Say, from what master didst thou learn the art
To charm, by words, which yet are mysteries?
Meseem'd as though I trod some path alone,
Which I had never trod before; and yet
All seems to me—all, all that thou hast said—
So godlike, so enchanting! Oh, speak on—
Yet no, speak not! Rather let me in thought
Linger along the words which thou hast spoken,
That mingled pain and rapture in my soul!

    (*Enter* GEOFFREY *hurriedly*.)

Geoffrey.
I see men at a distance coming hither!
Do not forget that we are here alone.

Tristan (*to* Iolanthe).
Now, noble maiden, must I take my leave.

Iolanthe.
Ah, no! no! Wherefore wilt thou go?

Tristan.
          I'll come
Again, and soon—to-day I'll come again.
Wilt thou permit me with thy hand to mark
How high I am, that, when we next shall meet,
Thou may'st distinguish me?

Iolanthe.
        What need of that?
I know that few resemble thee in height.
Thy utterance comes to me as from above,
Like all that's high and inconceivable.
And know I not thy tone? Like as thou speakest
None speak beside. No voice, no melody
I've known in nature, or in instrument,
Doth own a resonance so lovely, sweet,

So winning, full, and gracious as thy voice.
Trust me, I'll know thee well amidst them all!

TRISTAN.

Then fare thee well, until we meet once more!

IOLANTHE.

There—take my hand! Farewell! Thou'lt come again—
Again, and soon?—Thou know'st I wait for thee!

TRISTAN (*kneels, and kisses her hand*).

Oh, never doubt that I will come again.
My heart impels me hither. Though I go,
Still of my thoughts the better half remains;
And whatsoe'er is left to me of life
Yearns back to thee with evermore unrest.
Farewell!

(*Exit through the concealed door, following* GEOFFREY, *who has retired during the last speech.*)

IOLANTHE.

Hark! there he goes! Among the hills,
From which so oft the stranger's foot resounds,
Now echoes his light step. Oh, hush! hush! hush!
I hear it now no more.—Yes; there again!
But now,—'tis gone!—Will he indeed return?

If he, too, like so many guests before,
Should come but this one time! Oh! no—no—no!
Did he not promise me, and pledge his vow,
He would come back to-day? The dews are falling;
Already eve draws on.—Ah, no! to-day
He cannot come.—Perhaps to-morrow, then?
But now it is so lonely here.

FIFTH SCENE.

IOLANTHE, MARTHA, *afterwards* KING RENÉ *and* EBN JAHIA, *then* ALMERIK.

MARTHA (*enters from behind the house, and advances rapidly on seeing* IOLANTHE).

Dear child!
Great Heav'n! How came you thus awake, and here?

IOLANTHE.

Oh, Martha, come to me! Where have you been?

MARTHA.

Afield, among the servants. But explain:
Who—who awoke you?

IOLANTHE.

Of myself I woke.

MARTHA.

How! Of yourself?

IOLANTHE.

No otherwise know I.
But list—as yet you know not:—here have been
Strange guests!

MARTHA.

You mock me! Who were they?

IOLANTHE.

Two strangers whom I did not know at all,
And who, besides, were never here before.
It was such pity you had gone away!

MARTHA.

You dream, my child. Two strangers? Whence,
    and how?
It cannot be!

IOLANTHE.

Whence did the strangers come?
I ask'd not that; for you have charged me oft,
That I with questionings should not torment
Our visitors.

MARTHA.

Who were they, then, my child?

IOLANTHE.

Indeed, I do not know.

MARTHA.

Were you alone, then?

IOLANTHE.

I call'd on you, but yet you heard me not.

MARTHA (*aside*).

Heavens! was it possible?—(*Aloud.*) Say on, my child!

IOLANTHE.

Ah, Martha, none e'er came to us before,
Like these two strangers—like, at least, to one.
It cannot surely be, but that he comes
From some fair land of marvel, different quite
From this our land. For potent was his speech,
Yet gentle and affectionate as thine.

(KING RENÉ *and* EBN JAHIA *enter unobserved through the concealed door, and remain listening in the background.*)

He gave me greeting with a song. Oh, Martha!
A song that teem'd with meanings marvellous;

It charm'd the tears into mine eyes, although
I scarcely fathom'd half of what it meant.

MARTHA.

Be calm, my love!—(*Aside.*) What am I doom'd to hear?
(*Aloud.*) But tell me, pray, of what he spoke with thee.

IOLANTHE.

Of much—oh, much! to me both new and strange;
Knowledge had he of many, many things
Whereof before I never heard. He said—
Yet I, alack! could comprehend him not—
He said, we could distinguish many things
With—with the help of sight.

MARTHA (*aside*).

     Oh, God!

IOLANTHE.

       Dost thou
Know what he meant by this?

MARTHA (*observes the* KING *and* EBN JAHIA).

     Great Heaven! the King!

RENÉ (*advances*).

My child!

IOLANTHE (*falling on his neck*).

My own beloved father, art thou here?

RENÉ.

Thy tutor, Ebn Jahia, comes with me.

IOLANTHE.

He too! Where is he? Let me give you welcome!

(EBN JAHIA *gives her his hand.*)

RENÉ (*takes* MARTHA *aside, while* EBN JAHIA *converses with* IOLANTHE).

What has occurred?

MARTHA.

O God! I do not know.
In full reliance that she could not wake
Till she was waken'd up, we left the house
While she lay sleeping. But the while—so she
Maintains, although 'tis scarcely possible—
Some stranger has been here, and talk'd with her.

RENÉ.

Imprudent haste! When I went after him,
I did not mark to close the door behind me.
Well, Martha, and this stranger?

MARTHA.

                            He has spoken,
So far as I can gather from the maze,
Wherein she still doth wander, of her blindness.

RENÉ.

How! Of her blindness! Well, 'tis Heaven's decree
That she beforehand should be made aware!
So be it!—*(Beckons to* EBN JAHIA.) Ebn Jahia, hast
    thou heard?

EBN JAHIA.

This accident was fortunate indeed.
A stranger woke her. Here upon the table
I found the amulet. Yet what she heard
Of her condition is but dark to her.
I must require that she be fully told,
As you agreed.

RENÉ.

                My resolution's taken.

                        (*Approaches* IOLANTHE.)
Lend me thine ear attentively, my child!
No longer may't be hidden, that thy life
Hath reach'd a climax that will task thy firmness.
Wilt thou with patience hear me?—patiently,

If unexpected sorrow wound thy soul,
Learn to endure this sorrow?

IOLANTHE.

Father, say on!
It will be less severe, if from thy lips
It come to me.

RENÉ.

Then listen, Iolanthe.
I know not what the stranger said to thee;
Yet I surmise he told thee—what with care
We have till now conceal'd—that to thy soul
There lacks one potent instrument, to grasp
The world that round thee lies; and this is true!
For what thou lackest is the gift of sight.

IOLANTHE.

Ev'n so; and yet I understood him not.

RENÉ.

Then learn from me: there is a certain power
Which men do call the light. Like wind and storm,
It doth descend unto us from above,
And, like to these, with swiftness uncontroll'd,
The objects, which it touches, gain a new

Significance, and a peculiar stamp,
And oftentimes with warmth 'tis closely blent.
'Tis through the eye it finds its way to us,
And by the power of seeing it we gain
A true perception of the universe,
As it went forth from the Creator's hand,
And apprehend His wisdom and His goodness.
What thou by slow degrees and toilsome pain
Hast, until now, been forced to guess, the eye
Gives us to see and recognize with ease,
By its consistence and peculiar form.
(*With emotion.*) Early thine eye the pow'r of vision lost,
And this fair frame of earth, this radiant realm,
To thee, my darling child, was early closed ;
And all our care could scantily supply
The loss, which thou in infancy sustain'd :
All we could do was from thee still to ward
The shock and burden of intrusive cares,
And hide from thee their bitter origin.

IOLANTHE.

Ah, father ! These are wondrous words—to me
Incomprehensible. The universe,
How it came forth from the Creator's hand,

Knew I not that? Was this shut up from me?
How canst thou say so? My Creator, have I
Not recognized him in the universe?
Hath not the roaring blast, the zephyr's breath—
Hath not the warmth, that circles everywhere,
The earth's so fit arrangement, and its power
To nurture plants with blossom and with fruits—
Hath not stone, metal, and the flowing streams,
The choir of sweet birds' voices, shown me well
The great Creator in the universe?
And have I not by thee, ev'n as by all
That's dear to me, been taught to comprehend
What our Creator with the world design'd?
Even I am an expression of his will.
Where'er I turn—in nature, in the speech
Of others, in the depths of mine own being,
In thoughts that spring from thoughts, an endless chain,
In all, to me the self-same voice resounds,
And of His glory loudly testifies.

RENÉ (*aside to* EBN JAHIA).

Ah, Ebn Jahia, this so lovely faith,
We have destroy'd it!

IOLANTHE.

     Explain one thing to me:
I with my eyes, it seems, should grasp the world.
Yon stranger, too, who lately was with me,
And whose strange words are stamp'd so deeply here,
He spoke of sight. What is it, then, to see?
Can I, O father, see his voice, which touch'd
My soul with joy and sadness? Can I see
With these my eyes the nightingale's thick note,
Whereon I've mused so oft, and vainly striven
To follow it in thought, away, away?—
Or is her song a flower, whose fragrant breath
I know, but not its root, and stem, and leaves?

RENÉ.

Oh, my dear child, each of thy questions fills
My soul with agony. Trust, love, to me,
And leave it to a happier time, to show
What now to thee must be inexplicable.
One thing, however, know: I have a hope—
The hope, which hath sustain'd me until now—
That yet thy sight may be restored to thee:
That thy dear eyes may open once again
To the glad sunbeams; and oh, grant it, Heav'n!

Thy noble friend and tutor, Ebn Jahia,
With his rare leech-craft hath been long preparing
The favorable hour to test our hopes.
Now is it come, my own, my darling child!
Confide in him. Go with him to the house.
Martha shall wait upon thee.—At the first
Thou'lt sink into a slumber;—and from that—
If so it be Heaven's gracious will—aroused——

    (*Is stifled with emotion.*)

IOLANTHE.

What ails thee, father? Wherefore shakes thy hand?
My own dear father, joy'st thou not, that now
The hour has come thou'st panted for so long?
Thou fearest it will prove unfortunate.
Yet, even then, shall I not be, as ever,
Thy child, thy own dear child—thy child, who joys
To be so dear—joys in her happy lot!—
Let me go in, then——

RENÉ.

   Oh, my child! my child!

IOLANTHE.

Nay, do not fear! For what my sage kind master
Has ponder'd well, will prosper, I am sure.

It feels to me as though ev'n now I knew
The singular power which thou hast call'd the light,
And it hath found its way to me already.
Ah, while that wondrous stranger was beside me,
A feeling quiver'd through me, which I ne'er
Had known before; and every word he spoke
Resounded like an echo in my soul,
With new and unimagined melodies.
—Didst thou not say, the power of light is swift,
And gives significance to what it touches?
That it is also closely blent with warmth—
With the heart's warmth? Oh! I know it is.
If what thou call'st the light consist in this,
Then a forewarning tells me it will be
Reveal'd to me to-day. Yet on one point
Thou dost mistake. 'Tis not the eye that sees;
Here, close beside the heart, our vision lies;
Here is it seated in remembrance sweet,
A reflex of the light that pierced my soul,
The light I go with bounding hope to meet!

(*Exit into the house with* MARTHA.)

RENÉ (*to* EBN JAHIA, *who is about to follow*).

Stay, Ebn Jahia! Canst understand all this?

Where is the stranger, who intruded thus
Upon her bosom's peace ? How to myself
Can I explain these passion-laden words ?
What thinkest thou ?

     EBN JAHIA.

     Not easily explain'd
Is the full climax of a woman's mood,
And this, I own, goes counter to my plans.

     RENÉ.

Explain thyself !

     EBN JAHIA.

     Suppose her thoughts are bent
To rest upon this stranger—then, 'twould seem
That he controls her, and I strongly doubt
A happy issue to my art. And yet
In this conjuncture two desires may meet,
Which, blent in intimate communion, may
Strive to one end with like intensity.
In this hope I may rest—but only feebly.

     (*Exit into the house.*)

     RENÉ.

Who could it be, was here ? Unless Bertrand

Should chance to know——

(*Enter* ALMERIK *through the concealed door.*)

My Almerik! Thou here?

ALMERIK.

I bring a letter for my liege.

RENÉ.

From Tristan?

(*Breaks open the seal.*)

It is from him. What do I see? Come hither!
He breaks with me. He wishes to undo
Our solemn contract!

ALMERIK.

How! Undo the contract?

RENÉ (*reading*).

Amazement! He admits him in the wrong,
And leaves me to dictate the amends;
Yet—he repudiates my daughter's hand.

ALMERIK.

Matchless audacity!

RENÉ.

Ah, Almerik,
This is the fate that dogs me evermore.

An evil portent this, I fear me much,
For what this hour may bring. These nuptials,
Whereon I had the fairest visions rear'd,
Unconsciously were wedded with the hope
That Iolanthe should regain her sight.
That hope is gone—a little time may see
The other crush'd. Yet no! I will not stoop
To foolish, fond lamentings! Let that come,
Which Heaven in wisdom hath ordain'd for us!
Who brought the letter?

ALMERIK.

One of Geoffrey's people,
Who said, that Tristan now was lodged with him.

RENÉ.

With Geoffrey? Well, there still, perchance, is hope.
Perchance he may——But yet——What noise is that?
The clash of arms resounding from the pass!

ALMERIK (*approaches the door*).

They force an entrance——

RENÉ.

Force? Injurious knaves!

ALMERIK.

A handful of our people——

RENÉ.

Out with your sword!
They shall not flout King René unchastised.

SIXTH SCENE.

KING RENÉ. ALMERIK. TRISTAN *in complete armor, with his train. Afterwards* GEOFFREY, *with his train.*

(*During the progress of this scene, the evening red spreads over the valley and the distant hills, and remains so till the close of the piece.*)

TRISTAN.

Give back! The force, that sought to keep the pass,
Has yielded to our arms. Do you surrender?

RENÉ.

How now! What man art thou, whose ruffian hands

With shock of arms doth desecrate this ground?
Stand, or my wrath shall strike thee to the dust!

TRISTAN.

Husband thy words, old man. I have no fears.
I do believe, this place is in the thrall
Of some unholy and malignant power,
Which keeps thee trembling, but gives nerve to me.
If that thou be'st a sorcerer, and dost hope
For aid from magic spells, despair thy charm.
For know, the pope did consecrate this sword;
This scarf was woven, too, by holy hands
Within the Mary Convent at Avignon,
And, 'neath this mail of proof, abides the will
To quell thee, as Saint George the dragon quell'd.

RENÉ.

Deluded man! what motive brings thee here?

TRISTAN.

Reply to me! Art thou this valley's lord?

RENÉ.

Truly I am this valley's lord, I own;
Nor ends my title there. But who art thou?

(*Enter* GEOFFREY *with his train.*)

GEOFFREY.

What do I see? King René!—(*kneels*)—noble king!

TRISTAN.

What's here? King René!

RENÉ.

Geoffrey, thou in league
With one that is thy monarch's foe?

GEOFFREY.

Your pardon!
He posted on before. I came too late.

RENÉ (*to* TRISTAN).

Yet tell me, who art thou?

TRISTAN.

My name is Tristan
Of Vaudemont; a name you well do know.

RENÉ.

How? Tristan! (*To* GEOFFREY.) Is this true?

GEOFFREY.

'Tis as he says.

RENÉ (*musing*).

And so 'twas you, belike, as I conclude,
Were here to-day already?

TRISTAN.

Yes, my liege;
Chance, not presumption, led me to this place.
I did not dream that you were ruler here.

RENÉ.

But say, what motive brings you back again?

TRISTAN.

You know it.

RENÉ.

Nay, I know it not.   Explain.

TRISTAN.

Can this be so?—Within this blooming vale,
Where all is marvellous, there lives conceal'd,
And its most foremost wonder, a fair girl,
Whose praise not all Provence's troubadours
Could chant in measures equal to her worth.

RENÉ.

And this fair girl, you say——   Continue, sir!

TRISTAN.

Upon my soul such impress deep hath wrought,
That I am bound her slave for evermore.

RENÉ.

And know you who she is?

TRISTAN.

No. Yet there's proof
Upon her countenance, and in her words,
Of high degree, and inborn nobleness.

RENÉ.

And have you noted not, that Nature, who
In all things else hath been so bountiful,
Left her one flaw?

TRISTAN.

Ah, yes, alas! she's blind!
Yet there doth flow within her soul a light
That makes all luminous which else were dark!

RENÉ.

And though you are aware that she is blind——

TRISTAN.

Yet, at her feet with rapture would I lay
The golden circle of my earldom down.

RENÉ.

Now, by the holy image in Clairvaux,
You are the rarest marvel of our vale!
You press in here with weapons in your hand,
To bear off that which hath for years been yours,
Yet which you now insultingly contemn.

TRISTAN.

How so, my liege?

RENÉ.

Know, then, that this fair girl,
Who took your heart a prisoner, is my daughter.

TRISTAN.

Your daughter, she?

RENÉ.

My daughter, my young count:
The same whom you, as this your letter bears,
Can in no wise consent to take for bride;
The same who raised in you dislike so strong,

That, but to 'scape from her, you were content
To quit your claims forever to Lorraine!
The same, moreover, whom you so have charm'd,
That I might almost doubt, if the poor girl
So lightly would abandon you.

     TRISTAN.

       My liege,
Thou wilt not mock me with so wild a joy!

     RENÉ.
'Tis e'en as I have said.

     TRISTAN.

      But why was she——

     RENÉ.
Shut up within this vale? Of that anon.
You little deem, my lord, that you are come
At a momentous crisis. Iolanthe,
My darling child, perchance, e'en while we talk,
Sinks into darkest night for evermore,
Or wakes to taste the glorious light of day.

     TRISTAN.
What sayest thou, my liege?

RENÉ.

               This very hour
Has the physician, Ebn Jahia, chosen
To see, if possibly—— (*Approaches the house.*)
                  But hush! methinks
There is a stir within. Keep silence, all!
She speaks! Oh, Tristan, hear! Iolanthe speaks!
Ah, are these sounds of pleasure, or of wail,
That murmur o'er my darling angel's lips?
—But some one comes.

SEVENTH SCENE.

To the others enter BERTRAND, *afterwards* MARTHA, IOLANTHE, *and* EBN JAHIA.

RENÉ (*to* BERTRAND, *who enters from the house.*)

           Quick, Bertrand! quick, and tell me,
How goes on all within?

BERTRAND.

        Alas! I know not.

She has awaked, and it is nearly over;
But I ran forth in terror.

(Enter MARTHA *hastily.)*

MARTHA.

She can see!

RENÉ.

How, Martha—see?

TRISTAN.

Oh, grant it, Heaven!

MARTHA.

Hush! hush!
She's coming forth.

(Enter EBN JAHIA, *leading* IOLANTHE *by the hand. He beckons to the others to retire.)*

IOLANTHE.

Where art thou leading me?
O God! where am I? Support me—oh, support me!

EBN JAHIA.

Calm thee, my child!

IOLANTHE.

Support me—oh, stand still!
I ne'er was here before—what shall I do
In this strange place? Oh, what is that? Support me!
It comes so close on me, it gives me pain.

EBN JAHIA.

Iolanthe, calm thee! Look upon the earth!
That still hath been to thee thy truest friend,
And now, too, greets thee with a cordial smile.
—This is the garden thou hast ever tended.

IOLANTHE.

My garden—mine? Alas! I know it not.
The plants are terrible to see—take care!
They're falling on us!

EBN JAHIA.

Cease your fears, my child.
These stately trees are the date-palms, whose leaves
And fruit to thee have been long known.

IOLANTHE.

Ah, no!

Indeed, I know them not!

(Raises her eyes towards the sky.)

This radiance, too,
That everywhere surrounds me—yon great vault,
That arches there above us—oh, how high!—
What is it? Is it God? Is it His spirit,
Which, as you said, pervades the universe?

EBN JAHIA.

Yon radiance is the radiance of the light.
God is in it, like as He is in all.
Yon blue profound, that fills yon airy vault,
It is the heaven, where, as we do believe,
God hath set up his glorious dwelling-place.
Kneel down, my child! and raise your hands on high,
To heaven's o'erarching vault—to God—and pray!

IOLANTHE.

Ah, teach me, then, to pray to Him as I ought.
No one hath ever told me how I should
Pray to this Deity who rules the world!

EBN JAHIA.

Then kneel thee down, my darling child, and say,

" Mysterious Being, who to me hast spoken
When darkness veil'd mine eyes, teach me to seek Thee
In Thy light's beams, that do illume this world ;
Still, in the world, teach me to cling to Thee !"

IOLANTHE (*kneels*).

Mysterious Being, who to me hast spoken
When darkness veil'd mine eyes, teach me to seek Thee
In Thy light's beams, that do illume this world ;
Still, in the world, teach me to cling to Thee !
—Yes, He hath heard me. I can feel He hath,
And on me pours the comfort of His peace.
He is the only one that speaks to me,
Invisible and kindly, as before.

EBN JAHIA.

Arise ! arise, my child, and look around.

IOLANTHE.

Say, what are these, that bear such noble forms ?

EBN JAHIA.

Thou know'st them all.

IOLANTHE.

Ah, no; I can know nothing.

RENÉ (*approaching* IOLANTHE).

Look on me, Iolanthe—me, thy father!

IOLANTHE (*embracing him*).

My father! Oh, my God! Thou art my father!
I know thee now—thy voice, thy clasping hand.
Stay here! Be my protector, be my guide!
I am so strange here in this world of light.
They've taken all that I possess'd away—
All that in old time was thy daughter's joy.

RENÉ.

I have cull'd out a guide for thee, my child.

IOLANTHE.

Whom mean'st thou?

RENÉ (*pointing to* TRISTAN).

See, he stands expecting thee.

IOLANTHE.

The stranger yonder? Is he one of those

Bright cherubim thou once didst tell me of?
Is he the angel of the light come down?

RENÉ.

Thou knowest him—hast spoken with him. Think!

IOLANTHE.

With him? with him?
(Holds her hands before her eyes.)
Father, I understand.
In yonder glorious form must surely dwell
The voice that late I heard—gentle, yet strong;
The one sole voice that lives in Nature's round.

(To TRISTAN, *who advances towards her.)*
Oh, but one word of what thou said'st before!

TRISTAN.

Oh, sweet and gracious lady!

IOLANTHE.

List! oh, list!
With these dear words the light's benignant rays
Found out a way to me; and these sweet words
With my heart's warmth are intimately blent.

TRISTAN (*embraces her*).

Iolanthe! Dearest!

RENÉ.

Blessings on you both
From God, whose wondrous works we all revere!

(*Curtain drops.*)

IMPORTATION OF BOOKS
(*TO ORDER,*)

OF ANY DENOMINATION AND IN ANY QUANTITY, FROM A PAMPHLET TO A LIBRARY, CAREFULLY AND PROMPTLY ATTENDED TO BY

LEYPOLDT & HOLT,

(451 BROOME ST., NEW YORK,)

American Agents of

TAUCHNITZ OF LEIPZIC,

AND

TRÜBNER OF LONDON.

TERMS OF IMPORTATION TO ORDER:

	New Books.	Second-hand Books.
FROM ENGLAND. Per Shilling Sterling,	35 Cents.	40 Cents.
FROM FRANCE. Per Franc,	33 Cents.	37½—40 Cents.
FROM GERMANY. Per Thaler, (@ 30 ngr.)	110 Cents.	120 Cents.

From other countries at proportionately low rates.

The above rates are understood to be payable in GOLD or in United States Currency, with the ruling premium on Gold on the day of delivery of goods. TERMS CASH.

Delayed payments will be subject to a proportionate advance in currency, in case the premium on Gold should be higher on the day of payment.

On receipt of $1 for postage, Messrs. LEYPOLDT & HOLT will send for one year, to any address in the United States, European Antiquarian Catalogues of books in any designated department of Literature or Science.

They will also send notice of important new and forthcoming works relating to any branch of knowledge.

They invite correspondence on bibliographical subjects, and will always be happy to furnish any information within their knowledge.

BOOKS PUBLISHED

BY

LEYPOLDT & HOLT,

451 BROOME STREET, NEW YORK.

Beethoven's Letters, 1790-1826.

From the collection of Dr. L. Nohl. Translated by Lady Wallace. With a portrait and facsimile. 2 vols., 12mo. Cloth, gilt top. $3.50.

In this collection of his private correspondence we have an interior view of the great composer—showing us what he was, what he did, what he suffered, and what was the point of view from which he surveyed art and life. Beethoven, in music, is quite as great a name as Milton's in poetry; and among the thousands who have been charmed, thrilled and exalted by his wonderful melodies, and who really appreciate the originality, creativeness and might of his genius, these letters cannot fail to find delighted readers.—*Boston Transcript.*

Mozart's Letters, 1769-1791.

Translated, from the collection of L. Nohl, by Lady Wallace. 2 vols., 12mo. With a portrait and facsimile. Cloth, gilt top. $3.50.

These letters have the charm of Mozart's loving melodies. They are not less gay and tender, not less tremulous with sensibility, and seem to let us into the secret of his felicitous ease in composition—the secret of a bird "Singing of summer with full-throated Ease.—*G. H. Lewes, in Fortnightly Review.*

Delightful volumes of the letters of Wolfgang Amadeus Mozart, the composer, that, like his music, are warm and bright, bespeaking the genial and loving spirit that has ever made Mozart a favorite. It is through a man's private letters, designed simply for the eye of affection, that we ascertain the true character. We seem to sit with him and hear his voice in generous bursts of musical fervor, or in social love, or in friendly regard and inquiry, experiencing a pleasure different, but still as great, as that we experience when listening to his grand compositions—*Boston Saturday Evening Gazette.*

Mendelssohn's Letters from Italy and
Switzerland. Translated from the German by LADY WALLACE. With a Biographical Notice by JULIE DE MARGUERITTES. 1 vol., 16mo. Cloth. Price, $1.75.

"In these letters, the playful, affectionate nature of the man sheds everywhere the loveliest radiance. A murmur of song seems to have run through all his letters. They are the converse of his Songs without Words; and we venture to predict that the Letters of Mendelssohn will become as classical as those compositions . . . It is seldom that we have inclination to speak of a book in terms of equal warmth. We must add that Lady Wallace has performed her part of translator in a manner beyond all praise."—*Parthenon.*

Mendelssohn's Letters from 1833 to 1847.
With a Catalogue of all his musical compositions. Translated from the German by LADY WALLACE. 1 vol., 16mo. Cloth. Price, $1.75.

"There is not a page in this delightful volume which would not yield matter of pleasure and instruction to the reader."—*London Athenæum.*

"We wish our religious societies would call out a few of the letters of this man and scatter them broadcast over the land: they would indeed be 'leaves for the healing of the nations.'"—*Atlantic Monthly.*

Life of Felix Mendelssohn Bartholdy.
From the German of W. A. LAMPADIUS, with Supplementary Sketches by JULIUS BENEDICT, HENRY F. CHORLEY, LUDWIG RELLSTAB, BAYARD TAYLOR, R. S. WILLIS, and J. S. DWIGHT. Edited and translated by WILLIAM LEONHARD GAGE. With portrait. 1 vol., 16mo. Cloth. Top gilt. Price, $1.75.

"The short but interesting life by Lampadius is still the best, the only life of real value.... With the letters for illustration, it will be impossible for any musical person to read it without interest."—*Dwight's Journal of Music.*

Immen-See. Grandmother and Granddaughter.
Two Tales from the German. 1 vol., 16mo. Price, 35 cts. The same on tinted paper. Cloth. Price, 75 cts.

"Graceful and Charming."—*London Athenæum.*

Life of Chopin. By F. Liszt. Translated from the French by Mrs. Martha Walker Cook. 1 vol., 16mo. Printed on tinted paper. Cloth. Price, $1.50.

"In spite of the trammels of words, it gives expression to the same subtle and ethereal conceptions which inspired the genius of Liszt as a musical artist. As a sketch of the life of the great composer, it possesses an interest with which few biographical works can compare."—*Tribune.*

Musical Sketches. By Elise Polko. Translated from the Sixth German Edition by Fanny Fuller. 1 vol., 16mo. Tinted paper. Cloth. Price, $1.75.

"Elise Polko is a very delicate prose poet, who reminds us somewhat of De La Motte Fouqué. She has an infinity of enthusiasm, and the dream-essays she has wrought out from the lives of those eminent in musical composition are many of them remarkably delicate, graceful, and beautiful. The book is finely translated, all the tenderness and simple pathos of the original being apparently fully preserved. Few collections of partially imaginative sketches have lately appeared so likely to please the lovers of this peculiar branch of literature."—*Boston Evening Gazette.*

Good-For-Nothing (Memoirs of a). A Novel of the German Romantic School. By Joseph Von Eichendorf. Translated by Charles G. Leland. With illustrated Title-page and Vignettes, by E. B. Bensell. 12mo., $1.50.

"If there is still left any one who still some traces of Eden inherits, we advise him, we urge it on him, to give himself the great pleasure of reading this charming book."—*Nation.*

"A fine old German story, full of quaint humor and sweet touches of nature."—*Springfield Republican.*

Crumbs from the Round Table: a feast for Epicures. By Joseph Barber. $1.00.

"A spicy and piquant book, as full of good things as an English pudding is of plumbs, with great gustatory wisdom to commend it."—*Boston Sat. Evening Gazette.*

Thackeray's Works. A Uniform Edition.

16mo., gilt top, claret-colored morocco cloth. $1.25 per vol. Half mor. $2.00 per vol.

Vanity Fair	3 vols.
Pendennis	3 "
Henry Esmond	2 "
The English Humorists	1 "
The Newcomes	4 "
The Virginians	4 "
The Four Georges; Lovel the Widower	1 "
Adventures of Philip	2 "
The Great Hoggarty Diamond; Book of Snobs	1 "
The Kickleburys Abroad; Rebecca and Rowena, &c.	1 "
Major Gahagan; Fatal Boots; Ballads.	1 "
Yellowplush Papers	1 "
Sketches, Novels by Eminent Hands	1 "
Memoirs of Barry Lyndon	1 "
The Fitz Boodle Papers; a Shabby Genteel Story, &c.	1 "
Men's Wives	1 "

Each work sold separately.

Charles Kingsley's Works. 16 mo.

(uniform with Thackeray). Oak-colored cloth, gilt top, $1.25 per vol. Half mor. $2.00 per vol.

Yeast	1 vol.
Westward Ho!	2 "
Two Years Ago	2 "
Hypatia	2 "
Alton Locke	1 "
Hereward the Wake	2 "

Each work sold separately.

Heinrich Heine's Pictures of Travel.
Translated by CHARLES G. LELAND. Fourth revised edition. 1 vol., 12mo. Cloth. Price, $2.25.

"Those who wish for a single good specimen of Heine should read his first important work, the work which made his reputation, the 'Reisebilder.'"—*Matthew Arnold (Cornhill Magazine.)*

Heinrich Heine's Book of Songs.
Translated by CHARLES G. LELAND. 1 vol., 16mo. Printed on tinted paper. Cloth. Price, $1.75.

Schiller's Complete Works in English.
Selected from the best translations by S. T. COLERIDGE, E. L. BULWER, MELISH, T. MARTIN, A. J. W. CHURCHILL, and others. Edited by CHARLES J. HEMPEL. 2 vols., large royal 8vo. Price, cloth, $7.00; half morocco, $9.00.

Schiller's Poems and Ballads.
Translated by BULWER. From the last London edition. With portrait. 1 vol., 16mo. Vellum Cloth. Price, $1.50.

The Poetry of Germany.
Selections from the most celebrated Poets, translated into English verse, with the original text on the opposite page, by A. BASKERVILLE. Fifth edition. 1 vol., 12mo. Cloth. Price, $2.00; half morocco, $3.00.

This work, embracing 664 pages, gives choice selections of more than seventy of the first German poets, including the latest writers, with a note of the birth and place of residence of each. Each poem is given in full, German as well as English, rendering the book invaluable to all students of the former language.

Four American Poems. The Raven. The Bells. Lenore. The Rose.
Metrically translated into German by CHARLES THEODORE EBEN. With the original text on the opposite page. 16mo. Price, 25 cents.

"So well has he succeeded in rendering them into German, that they read like veritable productions of Germany."—*Worcester Palladium.*

"Who Breaks—Pays." By the Author
of "Cousin Stella," "Skirmishing," etc. 1 vol., 16mo. Price, $1.25.

"Who Breaks—Pays," is a love tale, told with exquisite pathos and poetry. There is a freshness and originality about the book which give it a place among the standard works of the day."—*Publishers' Circular.*

Skirmishing. By the Author of "Who
Breaks—Pays," etc. 1 vol., 16mo. Price, $1.25.

"Every page tells: there is no book-making about it—no attempt to fill chapters with appropriate affections. Each sentence is written carefully, and the result is that we have a real work of art, such as the weary critic has seldom the pleasure of meeting with."—*The London Reader.*

Fanchon the Cricket. From the French
of George Sand. By M. M. Hays. 1 vol., 16mo. Price 50 cents.

"An acknowledged masterpiece, read and admired in every country in Christendom."—*New York Commercial Advertiser.*

Human Follies. By JULES DE NORIAC.
Translated from the 16th Paris edition by GEORGE MARLOW. 1 vol., 16mo. Price, 50 cents.

"One of the most readable things of the day,—is a good illustration of the French way of teaching common sense. *Sixteenth* Paris edition,—this is a sufficient comment on the ability of the Author."—*Boston Post.*

The Romance of a Poor Young Man.
From the French of Octave Feuillet. By HENRY J. MACDONALD. 1 vol., 16mo. Price, $1.25.

The Romance of the Mummy. From the
French of Théophile Gautier. By Mrs. ANNE T. WOOD. 1 vol., 16mo. Price, 50 cents.

www.ingramcontent.com/pod-product-compliance
Lightning Source LLC
Chambersburg PA
CBHW020128170426
43199CB00009B/681